10 WAYS TO BE A BETTER LEARNER

BY
JEFF COBB

Copyright © 2012 Jeff Cobb
All rights reserved.

ISBN: 1468102354
ISBN 13: 9781468102352

*To my first and best teachers:
my mother, Gwen,
and my father, Kenton.*

*And to the two most inspiring learners in my life:
Cy and Selah.*

Around the World, What Lifelong Learners and Educators Say About *10 Ways to Be a Better Learner*

"As an educator and lifelong learner, I think that Jeff Cobb does a tremendous job of showing how you can stretch your mind to its fullest potential. The ideas in this book are research-based and insightful, and I love his ideas on attaining a "beginner's mind" to become a learner who can affect the world in positive ways. We all know where we want to go - the challenge is how to get there. *10 Ways to Be a Better Learner* will make that journey easier."

- Moana Evans, E*ducator,*
San Diego, California

"Jeff Cobb has put together a fantastic tome that reinforces basic education techniques that are often overlooked. This book will not only teach you techniques to learn, but how to learn constantly."

- Chris Hutton, *student/blogger at http://liter8.net,*
Bloomington, Minnesota

"As a teacher I thought this was an excellent book. It contained a great many ideas for how to be a good student once you leave school. I would recommend this book to anyone interested in bettering themselves. It provides a useful framework for thinking about how you actually acquire knowledge. It is a quick read that is well worth it!"

- Chris Kunkel, *Teacher,*
Jersey City, New Jersey

"*10 Ways to Be a Better Learner* provides a snapshot for students and teachers about the way we need to use our brains and other resources to tap into a better future. So, tap into any chapter now and see the immediate returns. "

- Anthony Paine, *Educational Leader,*
Noble Park North, Australia

"Jeff Cobb has condensed the most important and interesting research on self-directed learning into a compact, practical manual. Spend a few hours with this book and you'll gain invaluable tools for thriving in the learning economy."

- Blake Boles, *author of College Without High School and founder of Zero Tuition College (www.ztcollege.com)*

"I love learning. I love trying new things I've never done before or trying to do something even better. Reading Jeff Cobb's new book, I found it to be an easy read that is enjoyable, well written, and relevant to anyone who is looking to enhance their learning skills. Learning is a lifelong journey we all must embrace."

- Soha El-Borno, *Freelance Writer, Montreal, Quebec*

"This book is an introspection and reminder for learning. It makes me review my own learning and my classes. It works in personal life as well. I would recommend it to my students."

- Austin Tsai, *Chinese tutor & personal growth worker, Taipei, Taiwan*

"Ingest *10 Ways to Be a Better Learner* quickly—you'll want to read it at one sitting—and then digest it at your leisure so as to gain the maximum benefit. This is powerful medicine, but it requires no spoonful of sugar. Jeff Cobb's short but pithy book wrests learning from the context of academia into the learner's patch. It covers a wide range of topics ranging from the use of blogs to taking care of the body. I would recommend it to anyone wanting to launch their own lifelong growth and development."

- William Lucas, *Lecturer, Learning Support, Otago Polytechnic, Dunedin, New Zealand*

Table of Contents

Introduction	ix
1. Adopt the Right Mindset	1
2. Cultivate Your Network	11
3. Ask Questions	19
4. Be an Active Note Taker	25
5. Set and Manage Goals	29
6. Practice, Deliberately	39
7. Be Accountable	47
8. Use Technology Better	55
9. Mind Your Body	67
10. Embrace Responsibility	73
Final Words: One Step At a Time	79
Bibliography	81
About the Author	85
Shift Ed: A Call to Action for Transforming K-12 Education	87

They know enough who know how to learn.

- Henry Brooks Adams [1]

---

[1] See *The Education of Henry Adams*, 2007, p. 287.

Introduction

This brief book began as a series of posts on my blog, *Mission to Learn*. Based on insights I've gained through working on the blog for a number of years, as well as on my ongoing work in adult continuing education and professional development, I would like to offer these thoughts on how to be a better learner. At the core is the idea that continuous, effective lifelong learning is more important than it has ever been, and yet many of us do not give much thought to how we can become better learners. I don't pretend to offer all the answers, but I hope the areas covered will provide nutritious food for thought and help you shape your own approach to lifelong learning.

WHAT IS LEARNING?

As you read this book, it's important to keep in mind that the term "learning" is used about as broadly as it can be. Many people use "learning" to refer only to the trappings of formal education: courses, classes, degrees, and so on. While these are facets of an approach to learning, they actually account for a relatively small percentage of our learning experiences. Most of our learning – as much as 80 percent by some estimates[2] – occurs informally, through interactions with

---

2 The percentages are open to debate. See a good discussion of the topic at http://www.knowledgejump.com/learning/hype.html.

Learning is the lifelong process of transforming information and experience into knowledge, skills, behaviors, and attitudes.

friends, family, and colleagues, the world around us, or as part of our own self-directed efforts. The insights and advice offered in this book certainly apply to formal education experiences, but they are intended even more for the wide range of less formal experiences we encounter daily. We have to rely upon ourselves – indeed, we have to train ourselves – to get the most value possible from these learning experiences.

My definition of learning (discussed in more detail on the *Mission to Learn* blog[3]) is this:

> *Learning is the lifelong process of transforming information and experience into knowledge, skills, behaviors, and attitudes.*

For additional resources related to this book, please visit http://www.missiontolearn.com/better-learner.

WHY DOES IT MATTER?

The desire to learn new things and the ability to be constantly learning have always been key factors in living a successful, fulfilling life, but in recent years, as a consequence of two other key factors – *speed* and *complexity* – it has become even more important.

Just consider how rapidly and extensively the world of work has changed. After thousands of years in which most work was connected to farming, it took roughly a hundred years for most of the developed world to transition to a manufacturing-based economy. The demands of this economy – both to do the work of manufacturing and to provide a food supply to support large numbers of people who no longer worked on farms – required the creation of a wide

---

3 Jeff Cobb, "Definition of Learning," *Mission to Learn* (blog), May 21, 2009. www.missiontolearn.com

We now live in what is not so much a "knowledge" economy but rather a "figure-it-out-on-a-daily-basis" economy. Or, more formally, a *learning economy*.

INTRODUCTION

range of entirely new jobs, and a significant change in the nature of the old jobs. As manufacturing spread and agriculture evolved, both became increasingly mechanized, and more complex and specialized in the types of labor involved. Just as importantly, with the broadened availability of public and higher education and continuing advances in technology, the pace at which new types of jobs emerged, at which these new jobs became increasingly specialized, and then at which the jobs either disappeared or adapted to yet more change, increased dramatically.

Today, a mere fifty years after the economic height of the manufacturing economy, both rural and industrial life are distant memories for most of us. For decades we have lived in what the prescient Peter Drucker (1969) dubbed a "knowledge economy" – one driven by service- and information-based businesses. Drucker's descriptive phrase, however, no longer seems precisely on the mark. "Knowledge" sounds too finite. "Master a body of knowledge and you are on your way," it seems to say. While there are professions where that may still be true to some degree, any recent college graduate can attest to the fact that those professions are becoming harder and harder to find. We now live in what is not so much a "knowledge" economy but rather a "figure-it-out-on-a-daily-basis" economy. Or, more formally, a *learning economy*.

In this environment, where the speed of change continues to accelerate and the range of opportunities and challenges expands daily, there really is only one path to thriving: *continuous, effective lifelong learning.*

So, to be a better learner is not an academic matter. It's not something confined only to our school and university days, or deferred until later in life when we retire (for those of us so fortunate) and we have more time. Knowing how to be a better learner is essential to practical, everyday life, and it is simply not "optional." I trust this book will be of some small help to those who recognize this truth and are dedicated to becoming better learners.

1.

Adopt the Right Mindset

Each of us arrives in the world with a particular genetic makeup, and as a result, innate advantages or disadvantages in how well we deal with life's opportunities and challenges. Each of us is also subject to outside forces that are largely beyond our control, such as whether we are born into wealth or poverty, or where we live the early years of our lives. Clearly, the children of highly intelligent, affluent parents have a leg up in life, yet again and again we see people who seem to have no particular genetic or economic advantages get ahead in the world. Why is this?

Carol Dweck, professor of psychology at Stanford University, has spent years researching what differentiates people who achieve and maintain success. She's boiled it down to a simple dichotomy – individuals have either a *growth* mindset, or a *fixed* mindset. Consistently successful people have a *growth* mindset – a belief that they can *always* learn, grow, and become better at whatever they set their sights on. This is in contrast to the *fixed* mindset that holds so many people back – a belief that whatever talents or abilities one has are basically innate and not changeable to any significant degree. Success, it would appear, is fundamentally connected to and a consequence of learning, and *those who learn best are those who believe they can learn*.

A particularly powerful conclusion of Dweck's work is that simply being *conscious* of the dichotomy between the growth and fixed mindsets can make a tremendous difference. In *Mindset:*

> To learn and to grow, we must consciously tune into the opportunities that are around us, as well as the barriers that may be unnecessarily holding us back.

The New Psychology of Success, Dweck writes that:

> Just by knowing about the two mindsets, you can start thinking and reacting in new ways. People tell me they start to catch themselves when they are in the throes of the fixed mindset – passing up a chance for learning, feeling labeled by a failure, or getting discouraged when something requires a lot of effort. And then they switch themselves into the growth mindset – making sure they take the challenge to learn from failure, or continue their effort (Dweck 2008, 216).

I've emphasized the importance of *consciousness* again and again on the *Mission to Learn* blog. To learn and to grow, we must consciously tune into the opportunities that are around us, as well as the barriers that may be unnecessarily holding us back. Those of us who self-identify as lifelong learners already do this to a significant degree; we already embrace the idea of the growth mindset even if we've never heard it called by this name. But it's important to recognize that we bring different mindsets to different circumstances. Even the avid learner may have many areas in her life where a fixed mindset rules. One key to becoming a better learner is to ferret out these fixed mindset areas, and where appropriate, replace them with a growth mindset.

I say "where appropriate" because the goal is not to try to grow and change at *all* times in *all* aspects of life – that would be exhausting. But in the areas that feel most meaningful to us, where we feel motivated to put in time and effort regardless of external rewards like money or recognition, a growth mindset can be particularly powerful. *Believing* we can improve and excel tends to create a self-fulfilling prophecy; little by little we become more competent, and as psychologist Edward Deci has established, this feeling of competency leads to a sense of satisfaction and fuels our intrinsic motivation. "The 'rewards' linked to intrinsic motivation," Deci writes in *Why We Do What We Do*, "are the feelings of enjoyment and accomplishment

BELIEVING WE CAN IMPROVE AND EXCEL TENDS TO CREATE A SELF-FULFILLING PROPHECY; LITTLE BY LITTLE WE BECOME MORE COMPETENT.

that accrue spontaneously as a person engages freely in the target activities."

> Thus, feeling competent at the task is an important aspect of one's intrinsic satisfaction. The feeling of being effective is satisfying in its own right, and can even represent the primary draw for a lifelong career. People realize that the more they invest in a job, the better they will get at it, and thus the more intrinsic satisfaction they will experience. (Deci and Flaste 2008, 63)

Ironically, while the growth mindset and the achievement it fuels usually benefit from planning, goals, and rewards, at its core it is not about these things. It is about openness, curiosity, and a willingness to take risks and try new things. To borrow from the ideas of Zen master Shunryu Suzuki, having a "beginner's mind" is the key to learning:

> in the beginner's mind, there is no thought, "i have attained something." All self-centered thoughts limit our vast mind. When we have no thought of achievement, no thought of self, we are true beginners. Then we can really learn something. (Suzuki 2008, 22)

Suzuki's concept, rooted in Eastern philosophy, is not dissimilar from psychologist Mihály Csíkszentmihályi's scientific investigations into the mental state he has labeled "flow." For Csíkszentmihályi, "flow" is the state we achieve as we stretch ourselves in practice and focused attention and essentially "lose" ourselves in the task at hand. "Flow" is the ultimate learning state, and I would argue that the growth mindset is at its root.

THERE IS NOT MUCH JOY IN LIVING AND LEARNING IF WE DON'T TAKE TIME TO ACKNOWLEDGE THE THINGS WE HAVE DONE RIGHT – AND BUILD UPON THEM.

REFLECTIONS ON REFLECTION

A willingness to reflect regularly on life and learning is integral to maintaining the right mindset. If you don't currently make reflection a daily habit, I strongly recommend you try it. Here are some of the ways reflection can impact your life and your learning:

- **It helps you learn from – and get past – your mistakes.** "I have not failed, I've just found 10,000 ways that won't work," Thomas Edison is often quoted as having said. You can bet that Edison spent time reviewing his mistakes and failures; he did so to find his way forward to future successes.

- **It helps you learn from – and celebrate – your successes.** We can and should learn from our mistakes and failures, but there is also evidence that we may learn more from our successes (see, for example, http://bit.ly/learn-from-success). In any case, there is not much joy in living and learning if we don't take time to acknowledge the things we have done right – and build upon them.

- **It helps you make connections and solidify your knowledge.** A key part of acquiring and retaining knowledge is connecting it to things we already know. Conscious reflection supports this process and helps us get full value from our learning experiences.

- **It gives you perspective and helps you relax.** So many of us have lives that are overly busy and flooded by a continual stream of new information. We make mistakes, get overwhelmed, succumb to stress. Taking a few minutes daily to reflect, though, has an incredibly calming effect. It can help us put all of our efforts into perspective. Living and learning do not have to be about some grand, ultimate goal. Living and learning can be their own rewards. Relax.

Living and learning do not have to be about some grand, ultimate goal. Living and learning can be their own rewards. Relax.

HOW TO MAKE REFLECTION A DAILY HABIT
If reflection is something you'd like to practice more, consider making it a habit. Here are some suggestions for doing that:[4]

MAKE A COMMITMENT
Nothing becomes a habit if you are not willing to consciously commit to it. We all know instinctively that reflection is a good idea, but it's too easy to procrastinate and put it in the "Someday" bucket. Tell yourself clearly and consciously that you will make reflection part of your daily life.

FIGURE OUT WHAT WORKS
Reflection can take many, many forms. Take some time to find the one that is right for you. Here are just a few suggestions:

- **Sit quietly** for several minutes, perhaps doing some simple breathing exercises (see, for example, http://bit.ly/breathing-exercises).

- **Start a one-sentence journal.** This one comes from *The Happiness Project* blog (http://bit.ly/one-sentence-journal). Write one sentence (or thereabouts) a day. You'll be amazed at what you have captured by the end of a year.

- **Blend reflection with exercise.** This doesn't work for everyone, but runners in particular seem to be able to make it work. (Personally, I need to slow down a bit and walk if I am going to reflect while exercising – which I often do.)

Focus on doing it at the same time, every day. No exceptions. No matter which approach you choose, get into the reflection habit by taking just a few minutes at the same time each day to reflect. Do it in the way that works for you, but however you go about it, make sure you establish a "trigger" (such as, "right after I brush my teeth"). This will help establish the habit. It may even help to sign up for an online service that sends you a daily reminder at the same time each day (see, for example, http://www.memotome.com).

---
4 This section originally appeared as part of my "Zen Learning Habits" series and was inspired by Leo Babauta's "5 Powerful Reasons to Make Reflection a Daily Habit, and How To Do It."

2.

CULTIVATE YOUR NETWORK

If, as is likely, you found this book on the Web, you already have direct experience with the power of networks when it comes to learning. The Web gives us tremendous leverage; it makes it possible to tap into the thinking of others almost instantly and add to our knowledge more rapidly than has ever been the case before. In an increasingly complex, fast-paced world the ability to find, create, or take advantage of learning networks is more important than ever. We have to rely on others if we truly want to expand our potential for learning.

George Siemens and Stephen Downes, two thought leaders in the field of learning and technology, have termed the way in which we now acquire and manage knowledge "connectivism," based on the idea that "knowledge is distributed across a network of connections, and therefore...learning consists of the ability to construct and traverse those networks" (Downes 2011). Therefore, it makes sense that one of the most important strategies for increasing our capacity as learners is to build a significant number of connections with others, and more importantly, to strive consciously to make the *quality* of these connections as high as possible. Three factors take priority when assessing potential additions to my own learning networks:

Content

Is the connection a source of content that is consistently relevant and useful to me? Does the content help me to

In an increasingly complex, fast-paced world the ability to find, create, or take advantage of learning networks is more important than ever. We have to rely on others if we truly want to expand our potential for learning.

accomplish something? Does it stretch my thinking in meaningful ways?

Integrity

Is the connection trustworthy? Does the connection have the knowledge and experience to provide quality content? What is the quality of the connection's network?

Diversity

Does the connection represent a viewpoint that is different in some meaningful way from my own? Or, if similar, will it add to my own by being significantly further along in knowledge and understanding?

Of course, there are other possible factors and other questions that can be asked about each – you should adapt and add to the above considerations to suit your needs. The key point is to be *conscious of the factors* that make a learning connection valuable to you and to *apply these factors actively* in managing your learning networks. Sometimes that means using them to find new connections; often it means using them to prune connections that do not have significant value. It's truly a matter of *cultivating*, not simply growing.

It is important to note that the term "network" is not limited to connections made using technology. We all have networks that, while possibly enhanced by technology, do not require technology. Our family, friends, co-workers, and colleagues in civic organizations or trade and professional organizations represent just a few examples.

Technology is addressed later in the book, but the focus before technology comes into play should be on the actual points of connection – in network-speak, the "nodes"– and working to increase the quality of those points.

BE *CONSCIOUS OF THE FACTORS* THAT MAKE A LEARNING CONNECTION VALUABLE TO YOU AND TO *APPLY THESE FACTORS ACTIVELY* IN MANAGING YOUR LEARNING NETWORKS.

Finally, nothing here is meant to imply that you should take a cold, ruthless approach to managing your networks. Personally, I think networks and learning both benefit from a significant amount of chaos and complexity. Nonetheless, within all that chaos and complexity, you can strive to carve out and build upon a set of key connections that contribute significantly to your focused learning efforts.

A CURATOR IS AN INDIVIDUAL OR ORGANIZATION WHO EXCELS AT HELPING OTHERS *MAKE SENSE.*

THE CURATOR CONCEPT

One key to effectively tapping networks is to find good "curators" within those networks. There is such a flood of new content pouring through the Internet pipes these days that being aware of all of it and sorting it out in meaningful ways on your own is simply not possible. Curators are people or organizations that do the hard work of sifting through the content within a particular topic area or "meme" and pulling out the things that seem to make most sense.

This effort involves significantly more than finding and regurgitating links. A good curator must be skilled at:

- locating and evaluating valuable content
- organizing and connecting content so that it is as accessible as possible
- creating and re-purposing content when it adds to the underlying value
- capitalizing on the social web to build connections and context
- building trusted relationships with learners and other curators
- designing learning experiences (in a much broader sense than traditional approaches)

Bottom line: A curator is an individual or organization who excels at helping others *make sense*.

Finding good curators requires work, but some good first steps include searching blogs using Google's blog search (http://www.google.com/blogsearch) and Twitter using its search functionality (http://search.twitter.com). Determine who seems to be posting frequently and in valuable ways on topics you care about, and subscribe to or follow these people. Over time, they are likely to lead you to other people and other resources. You will no doubt need to trim some as you go along to prevent overwhelming yourself with too many information sources, but with a little effort, some initial searching for curators can result in connections to a highly valuable knowledge network.[5]

---

[5] The term "curator" has been a buzzword in various circles since at least 2007. I first came across it in George Siemens' thoughts on curatorial teaching at http://bit.ly/curator-concept.

3.

Ask Questions

Have you ever attended a class or seminar and when the time came for participants to ask questions, only one or two hands were raised (if any) – in a room with dozens of people present?

Have you ever read an inflammatory newspaper article, blog entry, Facebook wall post, or tweet, and not submitted a question about the "facts" it contains, or the author's sources and motivations?

Have you ever gone through a day, a week, a month, or even more at work without stopping to ask "why" (http://bit.ly/m2l-ask-why) about what you're doing and what you've learned (http://bit.ly/m2l-what-learned) in the process?

Have you ever voted in an election without examining who the candidates are and whether the issues they stand for are the ones that deserve priority?

    I could go on, but you get the point. We often don't take the many opportunities for asking questions that should, or do, occur to us. Most of the time that's fine: as previously noted, it can be exhausting to question everything. But I think there is plenty of evidence that most of us, most of the time, are not asking enough questions – especially good ones.

If you want to be a better learner, you have to cultivate – daily and consciously – both the desire and the ability to ask questions. It's that simple, and that hard.

As I've pointed out on the *Mission to Learn* blog, toddlers have no problem asking lots of questions (http://bit.ly/m2l-toddlers), but as we age, life demands, social pressures, and just plain fatigue tend to sap our desire and ability to continually probe, particularly outside of the comfort zones into which we inevitably settle. If you want to be a better learner, you have to cultivate – daily and consciously – both the desire and the ability to ask questions. It's that simple, and that hard.

The aim, of course, is not simply to ask more questions, but also to ask better questions, questions that are truly effective in advancing our learning. As a general rule, a good question should support our learning in at least one of four key areas:

1. RELIABILITY

How do you know that a new piece of information is true? What do you know about the source? Is the new information consistent with what you already know to be true? With the rise of the Web, and the consequent ability for nearly anyone to disseminate any information they wish, it has become more important than ever to establish the trustworthiness of new information.

2. SIGNIFICANCE

Why does it matter that the information is true? What is the potential impact of the information? How much time is it worth spending to learn more about or take action related to the information? Generally speaking, we need to understand why we should care about something before we are likely to make the effort to move it into long-term memory.

Learning is fundamentally a process of change. So, how will the way we act or think change as a result of new information?

3. COMPREHENSION

How well do we really understand the new information? What else do we need to help us make sense of it? How does it connect to what we already know? While we don't have to master the details of every new piece of information that comes our way, if we expect to remember it we do need enough depth to help us contextualize the information and relate it to things we already know.

4. ACTION

What *can* we do as a result of the new information? What *should* we do? Does the new information compel us to act differently? Learning is fundamentally a process of change. So, how will the way we act or think change as a result of the new information?

In many cases, we may find answers in each of these areas simply by taking a moment to pause and reflect upon new information as we encounter it. The point is not to become like a "teacher's pet" who always has her hand in the air, eager to ask a question simply to show how smart she is. The point, rather, is to be active in seeking answers, whether you do this out loud, on paper, or in your head.

4.

Be an Active Note Taker

While most of us are accustomed to taking notes during formal classroom learning experiences, we often don't do it well, particularly if (as is the case in most adult learning) we don't expect to be tested. Moreover, it is a rare person who applies the note-taking discipline of the classroom to the less formal, yet often more vital, learning experiences he encounters as part of day-to-day life.

Establishing a consistent habit of writing things down can be very powerful. A significant body of research supports the idea that simply writing something down contributes greatly to the process of moving it into long-term memory. As Françoise Boch and Annie Piolat note in their helpful overview of research on note-taking (http://bit.ly/notetaking-research),

> ...the result of taking notes is much more than the production of a passive "external" information store, as the note taking action itself is part of the memorization process and results in the creation of a form of "internal" storage.

But the initial act of writing things down is only part of the equation, if you want to leverage the full power of note-taking. For full effectiveness, notes need to be:

1. **organized** so that they can easily be accessed and reviewed
2. **reviewed multiple times** over time

Establishing a consistent habit of writing things down can be very powerful. A significant body of research supports the idea that simply writing something down contributes greatly to the process of moving it into long-term memory.

3. **re-worked** and **re-stated** in your own language
4. **reflected** upon
5. **connected** to your existing knowledge

As you can see, effective note-taking brings into play many concepts that we've already covered. Notes are not something simply to jot down and file away; they are to be returned to and actively mined over time.

There are a number of approaches to taking notes effectively, but one that has been broadly adopted is the Cornell method. The basic approach is to divide a page into three sections:

Key Words	Detailed Notes
	Summary

- a column on the right of the page for taking detailed (though concise) notes;
- a narrower column to the left for recording key words and phrases as you review the more in-depth notes you have recorded in the right column;
- a column across the bottom for writing a brief summary – usually a sentence or two – of the major ideas captured on the page.

The Cornell method is designed to support the five-step process above: organize, review, re-state, reflect, and connect. While originally developed as a method for taking notes during college lectures, it works well for most situations in which you need to capture and process information effectively.

Creating templates for taking notes using the Cornell method is simple (see, for example, http://bit.ly/notes-templates). *Lifehacker's* post on creating the ultimate notebook using the Cornell method is also worthwhile (http://lifehac.kr/rxTjsu).

5.

SET AND MANAGE GOALS

More often than not, we have only a vague notion of what we want to learn on any particular day, in any particular year, or over the course of our lives. And even if we can state it clearly – e.g., "I want to learn Spanish," or "I want to be a better manager" – we don't usually "chunk" our larger learning desires into manageable portions. Time passes – years, too often – and somehow we haven't achieved what we hoped. An obvious way to help is to set clear goals for learning. This is more than just a nice idea – there is plenty of evidence to suggest that, done correctly, goal setting can have significant positive impact on our performance in many areas of life – including learning.

In a review of 35 years of research on goal setting and motivation, Edwin Locke and Gary Latham (2002) identified four key ways in which goals affect performance:[6]

1. Goals help to direct our attention, both in our minds and in our behavior, towards what is most relevant.
2. Goals – particularly ambitious goals – help to energize us.
3. Goals – particularly hard to attain goals – help us persist in our efforts.

---

[6] In psychological literature a distinction is often made between "performance goals," actions necessary to achieve a desired outcome, vs. "learning goals," knowledge and skills required to perform. In short, learning is about process whereas performance is about outcome. When "learning" and "performance" are essentially the same thing – i.e., engaging well in the process *is* the desired outcome – my view is that the distinction does not apply.

❦

MORE OFTEN THAN NOT, WE HAVE ONLY A VAGUE NOTION OF WHAT WE WANT TO LEARN ON ANY PARTICULAR DAY, IN ANY PARTICULAR YEAR, OR OVER THE COURSE OF OUR LIVES.

❦

4. Goals lead us to draw upon knowledge we already have to perform actions or set strategies that support achieving the goal.

Most of us recognize intuitively that setting goals can help us learn more effectively. Of course, setting goals does not guarantee we will achieve them. In my experience, there are three key reasons for failing to achieve our targets:

1. A lack of rigor and specificity in setting goals

- We set **too many goals**. On the *Mission to Learn* blog I've highlighted a video from Franklin Covey (http://bit.ly/m2l-wild-goals) that stresses the importance of having no more than three "wildly important" goals at any one time. Beyond that number, the chances of achieving goals start to decline rapidly.
- We set goals at an **inappropriate level** – either too high or too low. The best goals require us to stretch beyond what is already familiar and easy, but are also designed to offer a reasonable chance of success (assuming we put in the required effort).
- We don't state **clear objectives** to support our goals. Objectives are the smaller, concrete achievements that lead to realizing our goals over time and are much more clearly measurable than goals. If you want to learn Spanish, for example, you will most likely need to set clear objectives around mastering verb forms, memorizing vocabulary, and engaging in conversational practice. Large, complex goals, in particular, need to be broken down into less complex tasks.
- We don't set – or track – clear **metrics**. If we are thoughtful enough to set objectives, we don't often set measurements for ourselves or *test* ourselves on our objectives. Can you pronounce and provide definitions for all the words on that vocabulary list? Did you spend 30 minutes in conversational practice this week?

THE BEST GOALS REQUIRE US TO STRETCH BEYOND WHAT IS ALREADY FAMILIAR AND EASY, BUT ARE ALSO DESIGNED TO OFFER A REASONABLE CHANCE OF SUCCESS.

In setting and tracking metrics, we get feedback on our overall progress towards the goal – and this feedback can then shape how we move forward.
- We don't set clear **deadlines**. Some goals can be wrapped up neatly – and for these we should clearly state "when." Others (as noted below) may never be fully achieved – but it should always be possible to put a timeline on the *objectives* that support a goal.

2. A lack of genuine commitment to goals

Stating a goal is one thing; truly committing to it can be quite another. Being rigorous and clear about your goals can help establish a true sense of commitment because you will have a more realistic perspective on what achievement of a goal will actually require. As Jeremy Dean suggests on *PsyBlog*, we've been conditioned by self-help literature to believe that positive visualization or fantasizing about success is one key to making achievement of our goals a reality (http://bit.ly/goal-fantasy). Research suggests, however, that we more authentically commit to a goal if we can clearly see the contrast between a positive future and our current reality, and then consciously embrace the work that it will take to move from the present to the future (http://bit.ly/goal-commitment).[7]

3. A tendency to treat a goal as a fixed outcome rather than a process

By its nature, achieving a goal tends to take time, and many goals defy completion in any definite sense. For example, if your goal is to be a great leader, when are you done? Even with more concrete goals, we tend to forget that the goal can be as much about the journey as the destination. This is yet another reason why objectives and measures are so important. It's all too easy to lose motivation when the top of the mountain is nowhere in sight, but by plotting out reachable points along our path

---

[7] It is important to note that conscious commitment does not require *public* commitment. While much advice about goal setting encourages sharing your goals with others, recent research suggests that doing this may actually be counter-productive. (See Peter M. Gollwitzer et al. 2009.)

WE MORE AUTHENTICALLY COMMIT TO A GOAL IF WE CAN CLEARLY SEE THE CONTRAST BETWEEN A POSITIVE FUTURE AND OUR CURRENT REALITY.

we maintain a sense of progress, and support the feeling of competence that can contribute to maintaining a growth mindset. The process of reflection (discussed earlier) is important here, to make it clear how much we learn along the way, even if achievement of the overall goal is further off in the distance.

A WORD OF CAUTION

As with most good things, it is possible to overdo it with goals. While research on goal setting as an aspect of self-directed learning is limited, various studies suggest that instructional goals set by teachers should not be *too* specific. When too narrowly focused, goals can limit learning.[8] A similar impact has been found in work situations. Employees are often burdened with too many goals, or goals that are too specific or short-term. While goal setting can seem like a panacea, it needs to be done judiciously. As a working paper from Harvard Business School put it:

> Rather than dispensing goal setting as a benign, over-the-counter treatment for motivation, managers and scholars need to conceptualize goal setting as a prescription-strength medication that requires careful dosing, consideration of harmful side effects, and close supervision. (Ordonez et al. 2009)

Again, this perspective is not focused specifically on lifelong learning, but it seems reasonable to expect that overly zealous goal setting could do as much harm as good for the individual lifelong learner. The following checklist, built on points covered in this chapter, should help with setting goals that are clear and measurable but also flexible:

1. **Keep your list short**
   Set no more than three significant goals at one time, and preferably fewer.

---

8   This is from work by Fraser (1987) and Walberg (1999) as referenced in "Setting Objectives," *Focus on Effectiveness: Research-Based Strategies, Northwest Regional Educational Laboratory*. 2011. http://www.netc.org/focus/strategies/sett.php

Goal Setting and Mindset

It is perhaps not surprising that goal setting can have an impact on mindset. In 2001, Seijts and Latham conducted a study to determine if goals act as a strong variable in learning. They drew on earlier work of *Mindset* author Carol Dweck regarding distinctions between performance goal orientation (PGO), which aligns with a fixed mindset, and learning goal orientation (LGO), which aligns with a growth mindset.

The study showed that individuals who have a high PGO but are given a specific and difficult learning goal perform as well as those who have an LGO. The bottom line: as a result of being assigned clear learning goals, both groups demonstrated growth mindset capabilities.

2. **Be ambitious, but realistic**
It helps to stretch when setting goals, but don't set yourself up for obvious failure.

3. **Be clear about point A and point B**
Be honest about where you're starting from and what it's going to take to get you where you want to go.

4. **Break it down**
Each step from point A to point B should be defined as a clear objective.

5. **Write it down**
Goals feel more real when you see them in writing. Whether documented on paper or digitally, make sure both your overall goal and your supporting objectives are in a place where you'll see them regularly.

6. **Set and track metrics**
You should be able to say, *definitively*, that you have completed work on objectives according to whatever schedule you set for yourself. Examples: *Practice scales for 10 minutes daily. Read 5 pages nightly. Write 3 pages per week.* Each of these has a number that you can shoot for.

7. **Record, review, reflect**
Keep a short, simple record of your daily activities and progress toward the overall goal. This helps make it clear that you are, in fact, making progress (or not), and it also serves as a tool for reflecting on your work, and as needed, adjusting your efforts or setting new directions for your goals.

6.

Practice, Deliberately

You may have heard the old joke about a tourist in New York City approaching a native and asking, "Pardon me, sir, how do I get to Carnegie Hall?" The New Yorker replies, "Practice, practice, practice!" More recently, you may have caught the buzz about the importance of "10,000 hours" of practice as popularized by best-selling author Malcolm Gladwell in *Outliers: The Story of Success*. The message in both cases is that if you really want to excel at something – or, at least, anything of substance and complexity – a lot of time and practice are required.

The "time" part seems straightforward, but I know from my own love/hate experience with learning the guitar (http://bit.ly/m2l-learning-goals) over many years that simply clocking hours of practice is not enough. The practice has to be of a certain quality.

The basic premise of *deliberate* practice – a concept that comes from the work of Swedish psychologist K. Anders Ericsson (2006) – is that not all practice is equal. As a result, two people putting in the same amount of time to acquire expertise may have dramatically different results. Deliberate practice is, well, deliberate – it involves not only repetition, but also feedback, reflection, and an intense focus on continuous improvement.

The bottom line: learning anything, whether a body of knowledge, a skill, or a new habit or behavior, takes practice. That practice needs to be deliberate if you want to achieve true mastery, or even if you just want to get farther faster.

> Deliberate practice involves not only repetition, but also feedback, reflection, and an intense focus on continuous improvement.

So what does deliberate practice look like? A 2010 article on "expert performance" in the *Strategic Entrepreneurship Journal* (Baron and Henry, 49-65) discusses eight key features of deliberate practice. While the authors focus on practice in the context of entrepreneurship, you don't have to consider yourself an entrepreneur to benefit from the insights, which apply broadly. With my own gloss on each, here are the eight key features of deliberate practice as discussed in the article:

1. **Deliberate practice is mentally very demanding, requiring high levels of focus and concentration.**
   You've heard it before: no pain, no gain. You have to be "fully absorbed" in your practice for it to truly be effective.

2. **Deliberate practice is designed specifically to improve performance—to strengthen it beyond existing levels.**
   You can't just put in time and expect to get significantly better at anything. You have to consistently stretch yourself, and then stretch some more.

3. **It must continue over long of periods of time.**
   As Malcolm Gladwell (drawing on Ericsson's work) suggested in his best-selling book *Outliers*, 10,000 hours – or approximately 10 years— of practice is needed to attain true expertise in pretty much anything of real substance. Better get to it.

4. **It must be repeated.**
   Even though repetition alone won't get you to the level of excellence, you also won't get there without it. Perhaps this is why the word "practice" is repeated three times in the old Carnegie Hall joke.

> You can't just put in time and expect to get significantly better at anything. You have to consistently stretch yourself, and then stretch some more.

5. **It requires continuous feedback on results.**
   Sometimes you can tell on your own whether you're doing things right. A wrong note on the piano, for example, tends to speak for itself. But very often this is an area where having a good teacher, coach, or mentor can make all the difference.

6. **Pre-performance preparation is essential.**
   This is where goal setting comes in – you have to know where you want to go if you expect to get there. Moreover, goal setting "should involve not merely outcomes, but also the processes involved in reaching predetermined goals" (Baron and Henry 2010, 65).

7. **It involves self-observation and self-reflection.**
   As you practice, you need to be continually aware of your own performance and focused on correcting and adapting as appropriate. This kind of in-the-moment self-assessment is critical regardless of whether a teacher is involved.

8. **Deliberate practice involves careful reflection on performance *after* practice sessions are completed.**
   In addition to being aware of your performance *as* you are practicing, you need to look back on it once you are done and determine where you stand with respect to your overall goals. What might you change to ensure ongoing progress?

It would be very difficult, if not impossible, to apply these eight points to all areas of our learning, but for the one or two areas we care most about and in which we truly want to excel, these eight points provide a useful roadmap.

Practice does lead to improvement, regardless of intellectual ability. So, while some may be satisfied with nothing less than greatness, there is a great deal to be said for a life of continuous growth and improvement.

SO, PRACTICE MAKES PERFECT?

While there is little doubt that continuous deliberate practice does improve performance, it may not be enough to enable the leap from good to great. Recent research suggests that the capacity of your working memory – the part of memory that actively processes new information as we encounter it – may be a more important factor.[9] Intellectual ability – of which working memory is a major component – does matter, and the jury is still out on exactly how much control we have when it comes to enhancing our natural intellectual abilities.

This may feel like bad news to some learners, but it is important to remember that practice does lead to improvement, regardless of intellectual ability. So, while some may be satisfied with nothing less than greatness, there is a great deal to be said for a life of continuous growth and improvement. Deliberate practice can certainly contribute significantly to that goal.

---

9   Dr. Zach Hambrick, associate professor of psychology at Michigan State University, notes, "While the specialized knowledge that accumulates through practice is the most important ingredient to reach a very high level of skill, it's not always sufficient." http://psychcentral.com/news/2011/10/06/key-to-greatness-is-working-memory-not-practice/30110.html

7.

Be Accountable

Too often we set out to learn something, but don't really hold ourselves to it. Here are three straightforward ways to make sure you hold yourself accountable for learning:

1. Check Your Sources

Take the time to check the facts and guard against unearned influence. Whether you set out to learn something purely for your own use or you plan to communicate what you learn to others (e.g., through writing about it or teaching it), the process of searching out and reviewing credible studies and perspectives on whatever the "something" is will help enhance your own learning through repetition and review, and will also help to ensure that you actually have it right. This is a very easy step to discount or overlook in our search-engine-happy world. It's easy enough to find someone willing to offer opinions – often positioned as facts – on pretty much anything.

A few clues that can help establish the authority of information include:

- **Credentials**
  Does the source of a fact or idea seem to have sufficient background (e.g., education, experience) to be a knowledgeable and reliable source?
- **Citations**
  Have others referenced it? How many others and in what types of work? Do the referrers seem trustworthy themselves?

TAKE THE TIME TO CHECK THE FACTS AND GUARD AGAINST UNEARNED INFLUENCE. THIS IS A VERY EASY STEP TO DISCOUNT OR OVERLOOK IN OUR SEARCH-ENGINE-HAPPY WORLD.

- **Corroboration**
  Are there other sources that provide additional evidence that a particular fact or idea is credible? Are the corroborators trustworthy?
- **Longevity**
  Has it withstood the test of time? Do others continue to cite it and corroborate a fact or idea months, years, or even decades after it first surfaces?

While none of these alone is reliable, a combination of two or more tends to be evidence of information that's pretty solid.

2. Test Yourself

If you want to move something into long-term memory, few methods are more straightforward and effective than testing yourself regularly *during* the process of learning. Occasionally, for example, I like to memorize poems (http://bit.ly/m2l-memorize-poems). When I am trying to memorize a new poem, I read it through a few times, put it aside, and then a bit later make myself try to repeat as much of it as possible from memory. In learning theory-speak, this process is called "retrieval," and you do much the same thing when you use flash cards to test your memory of new vocabulary, or force yourself to re-state the key points from a lecture or article in your own words (a practice suggested in the chapter on note-taking). If you want to get fancy, there are any number of tools on the Web for creating flash cards or putting together quizzes and tests. (See, for example, http://quizlet.com/ and http://www.proprofs.com/quiz-school/.)

If you want to move something into long-term memory, few methods are more straightforward and effective than testing yourself regularly *during* the process of learning.

A 2007 paper from Washington University describes this sort of approach as *test-enhanced learning*. "As you read text material," the paper's authors write:

> make up questions … and then later test yourself. If you can retrieve the information from memory, great; having retrieved it once, you will remember it even better. If you can't retrieve the answer, study the material again and retest yourself until you're sure you know it. But even if you were able to retrieve the answer once, don't stop. Test yourself repeatedly and keep retrieving answers. Repeated retrieval is the key to long term retention. (Roediger et al. 2007)

Among a variety of evidence the authors offer in support of test-enhanced learning, they cite an experiment in which three different groups of students were asked to read brief passages of text. The first group read the passage a total of four times but was not tested on it; the second read it a total of three times and took a short test only after having completed all repetitions of the passage; the third was tested three times – once after each reading of the test. When tested a week later, the first group had retained only about 40 percent of the core information in the passages while the second group retained more than 50 percent, and the third more than 60 percent (Roediger et al. 2007, 3-4). Clearly a little testing can go a long way.

3. Teach It
When you commit to teaching something, you become accountable not only to yourself but also to those seeking to learn from you. Preparing to teach involves many of the processes already described in this book, particularly those covered in deliberate practice. While you do not necessarily need to *master* a topic or skill to teach it, you typically do need to possess significant knowledge of it as well as a reasonable level of comfort and fluency in talking about it. Preparation and practice are really the only reliable path.

> When you commit to teaching something, you become accountable not only to yourself but also to those seeking to learn from you.

Opportunities to teach others are myriad. Simply posting to a blog, or sharing your knowledge and experience in social networks like Facebook or LinkedIn are informal forms of teaching. Or, if you want to be a bit more formal, post an instructional video to YouTube, take advantage of Web-based teaching sites like MindBites (http://www.mindbites.com/) or WizIQ (http://www.wiziq.com/), or check into teaching a course at a local community center or community college. The possibilities for teaching – and learning – are endless.

8.

Use Technology Better

It's easy to become overwhelmed by the wide range of lifelong learning options that technology has made possible. But given that people were able to learn long before the days of Google, TEDTalks (http://www.ted.com/), and Twitter, it's worth taking a moment to reflect on *how* technology enhances our natural learning capabilities and opportunities. This understanding can help us use technology for learning in more productive and beneficial ways.

There are five key ways in which technology boosts learning, and for each, I've also proposed some questions to help you improve your use of technology.

1. Assessment

By "assessment," I mean not simply traditional quizzing or testing (although certainly there are ways to test your knowledge on almost anything, ranging from quantitative aptitude tests (http://bit.ly/aptitude-test) to squishier topics like civic literacy (http://bit.ly/smktKD)). Rather, I think technology can be used in a broader sense to *gauge* what you need to know and at what level. You can get a sense of this by using search and other tools intelligently to track a topic (http://bit.ly/m2l-track-topic) and by listening in to the conversations you discover. And look out in particular for good curators (see chapter 2) in areas that interest you: these people generally provide very good clues as to what the baseline of knowledge is for that area as well as what is on the cutting edge.

It's worth taking a moment to reflect on *how* technology enhances our natural learning capabilities and opportunities. This understanding can help us use technology for learning in more productive and beneficial ways.

Questions to ask yourself:

- *Have I found tools that help me test the knowledge I possess in a particular area?*

- *Have I identified information sources, conversations, and curators that help me assess ways in which I might want to build my knowledge or skills?*

2. Access

There is no doubt that technology has dramatically expanded access to learning opportunities. In many cases the Web has all but eliminated time and distance as barriers to learning, and a great deal of what is available on the Web, from open educational resources (http://bit.ly/m2l-oer) to learning games (http://bit.ly/m2l-learning-games) to podcasts (http://bit.ly/m2l-podcasts) to millions of blogs, is free (http://bit.ly/m2l-free-learning). One challenge, of course, is that with so much available, it can be hard to know where to turn or how to focus (that's one reason why the curators mentioned above are so important). Effective use of technology for learning requires continuous reflection on your own learning goals (see chapter 5) and exploration of the types of content, experiences, and interactions that may be available. Ask yourself the following:

- *When is the last time I went on a "learnabout" (a coinage based on the term "walkabout") to find interesting new resources to support my learning goals?*

- *What are the types of technology-driven learning experiences I have found helpful, and why? Where can I find more of a similar nature?*

If we don't actively use technology to promote diversity we may succumb to homophily – a tendency to seek out only information and ideas with which we agree.

3. Diversity

Technology opens up the possibility of listening to and interacting with a much more diverse range of people and ideas than ever before. Since I started blogging in 2007, I've communicated with people from all around the world, and I have no doubt that doing so has enhanced my knowledge and understanding in a variety of areas. But certainly the opposite can easily be true as well: if we don't actively use technology to promote diversity we may succumb to homophily – a tendency to seek out only information and ideas with which we agree (see http://bit.ly/m2l-homophily). More questions:

- *Am I consciously using technology to seek a diversity of learning experiences?*
- *Do I repeat the same old things again and again, or do I challenge myself to find ideas and perspectives I haven't previously considered?*

4. Action

It's easy enough to read a blog post, watch a video, or tune into a podcast – all activities that can support learning – but technology also provides any number of opportunities for being *active* rather than *passive* as a learner, and for being not just a consumer, but a producer. For me, the *Mission to Learn* blog is an example – I have used it over the years as a way to explore ideas and consolidate my knowledge by writing about them. I have used podcasting (http://bit.ly/m2l-podcasting-guide) in much the same way. Whatever tools you prefer, there any number of ways you can use technology to review things you have studied, be an active note-taker, and create learning opportunities for others while learning yourself.

- *Am I using technology not just as tool for passive consumption, but also as a way to actively engage in learning activities, such as taking notes, writing a blog, playing learning games, etc.?*
- *What new approaches – e.g., creating a podcast, producing a short video, starting a Tumblr feed (http://tumblr.com) – might align well with my current learning goals?*

It's easy enough to read a blog post, watch a video, or tune into a podcast – all activities that can support learning – but technology also provides any number of opportunities for being *active* rather than *passive* as a learner.

5. Order

Technology gives us ways that we've never had before to manage information and learning opportunities. Personally, I think I'd be lost without an RSS reader (for example, http://www.google.com/reader/) for aggregating and organizing all of the many blogs I track. I channel some Twitter streams into RSS, but I also use the Web-based application Hootsuite (http://www.hootsuite.com/), which lets me easily organize people into groups or track particular hashtags (words preceded by a "#" sign on Twitter). And increasingly I use Evernote (http://www.evernote.com) as a way take notes and sync them across my laptop, iPad, iPhone, and the Web. I could go on and on, but you get the point. For more resources on the range of tools that can be used for organizing and tracking learning, see the section at the end of this chapter and also visit the resources page for this book at http://www.missiontolearn.com/better-learner/.

- *Am I using technology tools effectively to help me make sense of the chaotic flow of new information and experiences?*
- *Have I explored the full capabilities of the tools I'm using so that I can get the most out of them? (Hint: return to "Assessment" above for an approach to figuring out what you may need to know to use a particular tool effectively.)*

That's it. Naturally, there is an incredible array of technology tools available to help you leverage each of these five areas. An entire book could be written on that alone – but, of course, it would soon be out of date. The section that follows provides some of the tools that I currently find most helpful in supporting my own lifelong learning.

A DOZEN FAVORITE TECHNOLOGY TOOLS FOR LEARNING

The range of technology tools you can use to support and enhance your learning is truly amazing. The following list covers some of my favorites, along with brief notes on how I use them. Nearly all of these are available across multiple platforms – such as PC/Mac, iPad, iPhone, and Android.

1. RSS Reader

The free Google reader (http://www.google.com/reader) is probably the most important tool in my learning mix. I use it to subscribe to and organize information from a wide variety of blogs and Twitter feeds, with a heavy emphasis on tracking the writings of "curators."

2. Blog

I read a lot of blogs, but I also consider writing blog posts on a regular basis to be a key part of my lifelong learning. To write about something, you have to make sure you understand it well enough to put it into your own words – a surefire way to learn. I use free (and amazing!) WordPress software (http://wordpress.org) for most of my blogging, but a much more streamlined option I've also used is Tumblr (http://tumblr.com).

3. Twitter

While some people think of Twitter as "noise," I see it as valuable stream of real-time information and links to valuable resources. It's also a great tool for building your learning network. Free tools like Hootsuite (http://hootsuite.com) and Tweetdeck (http://tweetdeck.com) can help you better organize the people you follow into groups, or track hashtags (keywords that begin with a "#" symbol).

4. iTunes

I'm a podcast junkie, and I find iTunes (http://www.apple.com/itunes/) to be the easiest place to locate and subscribe to podcasts. Apple also offers the amazing iTunes University, where you can discover great free content on nearly any topic from top-flight universities. Finally, if you create podcasts (which I also do as part of my learning activities) you can easily publish them to iTunes. See my free Podcasting Guide for more information on how to create podcasts.

- http://www.missiontolearn.com/podcastguide/

5. Delicious

The Delicious (http://delicious.com) social bookmarking service enables you to save links so that they are accessible through any Web browser and can be shared with others. It's a great place to keep track of resources you find on the Web, and also to find resources that others have saved and tagged. You can see a good example at http://delicious.com/jcobbm2l/ .

6. Evernote

Evernote (http://www.evernote.com) provides digital note-taking software in both free and premium versions. Evernote makes it easy to capture and save notes – both written and audio – and most important for me, to sync them across multiple devices.

7. LinkedIn

I use search and the Groups functionality on LinkedIn a great deal when I'm trying to find expertise in specific areas related to my work. You can use Facebook in a similar way; I just happen to find LinkedIn more useful in my line of work. For a fuller discussion of how LinkedIn can be used for learning, see my blog post "7 LinkedIn Tactics for Lifelong Learning":

- http://www.missiontolearn.com/linkedinlearning/

8. Zite

Zite (http://www.zite.com) is an iPad application that leverages your Google Reader and Twitter accounts to create a personalized "magazine." The magazine becomes even more personalized over time as you indicate whether or not you like the articles it serves up. I've found it to be a great tool for continually narrowing in on the best sources for a small set of topics of most interest to me. Every time I launch Zite, the range of resources it presents becomes more and more relevant.

9. Instapaper

Often when I read through blog posts or Web pages, I come across great resources that are too lengthy to absorb right way. Instapaper (http://www.instapaper.com) gives me a great way to save them for later, when I have more time. Another option is the appropriately named "Read It Later." (http://www.readitlater.com).

10. SlideShare

People who speak at meetings, seminars, and other events are often a great source of information about particular topics. More and more, these people post their PowerPoint slides to SlideShare (http://slideshare.net), a site where you can easily upload, share, search, and comment on slides.

11. YouTube

YouTube (http://www.youtube.com) is now the second largest search engine behind Google (which owns it), and for good reason – it is home not only to many highly entertaining videos, but also to many highly educational ones. Sifting through them to find the gems can be a bit daunting, but if you want a great starting point, check out Open Culture's Smart YouTube Channels and Intelligent Video collections:

- http://www.openculture.com/smartyoutube
- http://www.openculture.com/intelligentvideo

12. Kindle

I don't yet own an Amazon Kindle (http://www.kindle.com), but I am nonetheless an avid user of Kindle software on my iPad. The ability to carry around and reference an entire library of books in a single, small device is of inestimable value to me. My hope is that over time Amazon will improve the already helpful capabilities for highlighting, taking notes, and sharing. If these become more flexible, Kindle has the potential for being a truly revolutionary learning platform.

9.

Mind Your Body

There is ample evidence that how we treat our bodies can have a significant impact on how well our minds function. If you want to learn better, it makes sense to support this goal with a good diet, adequate sleep, and plenty of exercise.

DIET

What we eat can directly impact how our brains function, and how receptive and capable we are as learners. An excellent article in this area is "Brain Foods: The Effect of Nutrients on Brain Function" (Gómez-Pinilla 2008), which I highly recommend you read in full (http://bit.ly/food-brain). For the time-challenged, however, here are a few highlights:

- Food is like a drug in many ways – it contains specific substances that can impact how the brain functions.
- Omega 3 fatty acids, found in fatty fish (such as salmon), flax seed, and walnuts, appear to help brain function and may even slow cognitive decline in the elderly.
- Saturated fats, found in dairy products, meat, and oily snack foods, can have a negative impact.
- Flavenoids, found in cocoa, dark chocolate, green tea, citrus fruits, and wine, may improve cognitive function, particularly in combination with regular exercise.

> What we eat can directly impact how our brains function, and how receptive and capable we are as learners.

- With respect to memory – a key element of learning – Gómez-Pinilla specifically mentions B vitamins as having a positive impact for women.

Gómez-Pinilla's article features a great chart that summarizes the effects of different types of food on the brain. The *Happy Healthy Long Life* blog (http://bit.ly/happy-healthy) has included the chart in an excellent summary it offers of Gómez-Pinilla's article. As the author notes, it's worth printing out and putting on your fridge.

SLEEP

A key goal for any learner is to "consolidate" learning by moving new information and experiences into long-term memory, and a wide range of scientific studies support the idea that sleep is essential for this process. A 2009 MIT study (http://bit.ly/sleep-memory), for example, brought us a significant step closer to understanding the sleep-memory connection by showing that "mice prevented from 'replaying' their waking experiences while asleep do not remember them as well as mice who are able to perform this function" (Halber 2009).

The bottom line: Sleep is important. Get enough of it if you want to make sure your memory is functioning properly.

Of course, that begs the question: *what is enough?* Unfortunately there is no "one-size-fits-all" answer to that question. The safest bet seems to be to aim for at least the standard 7-8 hours a night recommended for most adults, and to pay attention to how you feel and act based on that amount of sleep so that you can adjust up or down as needed. For more information on sleep needs from infants up to adults, i recommend an article on sleep requirements in *Parenting Science* (http://bit.ly/sleep-requirements).

THE BOTTOM LINE: SLEEP IS IMPORTANT. GET ENOUGH OF IT IF YOU WANT TO MAKE SURE YOUR MEMORY IS FUNCTIONING PROPERLY.

EXERCISE

Tracing a direct path between physical exercise and our ability to learn is a little tricky, but a significant body of research suggests that physical exercise may boost spatial memory, neuroplasticity, and other aspects of brain function essential to learning.

At a minimum, a short-term effect of exercise, and in particular aerobic exercise that lasts at least 30 minutes, is an increase in blood flow and corresponding oxygen supply to the brain. This can help boost cognitive function, including memory. A regular exercise habit can help to improve circulation in general and also ward off stress and depression – two established enemies of optimal cognitive function.

Research also suggests that physical exercise may directly benefit the hippocampus, an area of the brain that is essential to memory. One recent study showed that "elderly adults who are more physically fit tend to have bigger hippocampi and better spatial memory than those who are less fit." As one of the lead researchers on the study put it, "Basically, if you stay fit, you retain key regions of your brain involved in learning and memory" (Yates 2009).

So how much exercise should the average person get? There's plenty of debate on the topic, but one reasonable starting point is the Center for Disease Control's "How much physical activity do you need?" (http://1.usa.gov/how-much-activity)

Of course, in the end, the information in this chapter can only scratch the surface of how the way we treat our bodies can impact brain function. It's clear, however, that if you want to be a better learner, *it pays to take care of yourself.*

10.

EMBRACE RESPONSIBILITY

This book began by considering what we *can* do as learners if we believe in our capabilities for learning and growth and want to enhance those abilities. This final chapter considers what we *should* do. While learning is necessarily a highly individualistic activity, it always occurs in *context* and with *conditions* that the successful learner must take into account.

"Context" includes the social relationships and broader environment in which and through which learning occurs; "conditions" recognizes the many dependencies that are a part of learning, including the idea that more often than not, one thing cannot be learned without first learning another thing, or many other things. For a learner to recognize and take into account these factors is a form of responsibility that manifests in three major ways:

> ***1. The best learners recognize that their learning is not purely about themselves*** *– it is an ongoing part of being someone who is connected to and contributes to the world in positive, productive ways.*

The ability to contribute means having the capacity to engage with and help solve problems, both large and small, and having the capacity to help make the most of opportunities that arise throughout our lives. Contributing means doing these things as much for the positive impact they have on others and the world around us as for ourselves. There is

The best learners

1. recognize that their learning is not purely about themselves;
2. put in the effort to learn even when they may not want to;
3. *are dedicated to learning well and learning correctly.*

no way to do this effectively other than through constant, lifelong learning.

We are, of course, free to do otherwise. That's why this is a question of embracing responsibility: we must choose which path to take.

2. *The best learners put in the effort to learn even when they may not want to.*

We are not always motivated to learn the things we can and should learn, but the best learners do the necessary work regardless. It's rare that mastering all parts of a skill or a particular body of knowledge is enjoyable. A person who studies a foreign language, for instance, may be motivated by the idea of speaking fluently with the people of a foreign land, but not motivated at all to master the intricacies of grammar. The former, of course, won't happen without the latter. Similarly, we all have to learn a variety of rules and lessons that enable us to function collectively as a society. While these are typically imposed upon us, successful learners are able to integrate them productively into their lives.

3. *The best learners are dedicated to learning well and learning correctly.*

In *Democracy and Education*, John Dewey, one of the great philosophers of education, writes about responsibility as:

> …the disposition to consider in advance the probable consequences of any projected step and deliberately to think them through: to accept them in the sense of taking them into account, acknowledging them in action, not yielding a mere verbal assent (Dewey 1916, 178).

With conscious, consistent effort, we can improve dramatically. And each improvement makes the next one just a little easier.

Dewey's perspective extends the concept of accountability discussed earlier. It's very easy to be a passive learner or a lazy learner who simply accepts information and ideas as presented, or who shapes information and ideas according to whatever biases feel most comfortable or useful. Read or watch the news on any given day and you will see myriad examples of this sort of learning behavior. Consciously or unconsciously, people take shortcuts. They don't check the facts, do the work, or fully consider the consequences of not doing these things.

We are all free to take these kinds of shortcuts, but again – that's why this is a question of embracing responsibility. Those who choose to do the work learn "what is involved in really knowing and believing a thing" – and revel in it (Dewey 1916, 178).

Final Words: One Step at a Time

One of my mentors is fond of pointing out that, just like money in a savings account, the "returns" from learning tend to compound over time. As a result, if we make the effort to improve by just one percent each day, in seventy days we will be twice as good.[10] This is a perspective that every dedicated lifelong learner would do well to adopt. Even with a lifetime of effort, no one is capable of truly mastering all of the points discussed in this book, but bit by bit, with conscious, consistent effort, we can improve dramatically. And each improvement makes the next one just a little easier.

As you continue on your learning journey, I encourage you to pick just one or two of the points in this book to focus on for the short term. As you make progress, return to the book and identify the next set of areas you want to work on. Over time, you're certain to see your efforts produce more and more significant results. If you are occasionally discouraged or feel overwhelmed by how much there is to know, I'd encourage you to pause, reflect, and take heart in the words from Henry Adams with which this book began:

They know enough who know how *to learn*.

---

[10] The mentor I have in mind is Alan Weiss (http://www.summitconsulting.com). I don't know whether the "1% solution" is original to him, but I have heard him reference it many times in various seminars.

Bibliography

Adams, Henry B. *The Education of Henry Adams*. New York: Cosimo Books, 2007.

Babauta, Leo. "5 Powerful Reasons to Make Reflection a Daily Habit, and How to Do It." *Zen Habits*. Dec. 30, 2007. http://zenhabits.net/5-powerful-reasons-to-make-reflection-a-daily-habit-and-how-to-do-it/

Baron, Robert A. and Rebecca A. Henry. "How Entrepreneurs Acquire the Capacity to Excel: Insights from Research on Expert Performance." *Strategic Entrepreneurship Journal* 4, no. 1, (2010): 49–65. http://onlinelibrary.wiley.com/doi/10.1002/sej.82/pdf

Cobb, Jeff. *Mission to Learn* (blog), www.missiontolearn.com

Deci, Edward L., and Richard Flaste. *Why We Do What We Do: Understanding Self-Motivation*. New York: Penguin Books, 1996.

Dewey, John. *Democracy and Education: An Introduction to the Philosophy of Education*. New York: The Free Press, 1916.

Downes, Stephen. "Week 1: What is Connectivism." *Connectivism and Connected Knowledge 2011*. http://cck11.mooc.ca/week1.htm

Drucker, Peter F. *The Age of Discontinuity: Guidelines to Our Changing Society*. New York: Harper & Row, 1969.

Dweck, Carol. *Mindset: The New Psychology of Success*. New York: Ballantine Books, 2008.

Ericsson, K. Anders. "The Influence of Experience and Deliberate Practice on the Development of Superior Expert Performance." *The Cambridge Handbook of Expertise and Expert Performance*. 685-706. Cambridge: Cambridge University Press, 2006.

Gollwitzer, Peter M., Pascal Sheeran, Verena Michalski, and Andrea E. Seifert. "When Intentions Go Public: Does Social Reality Widen the

Intention-Behavior Gap?" *Psychol Sci* 20, (2009). http://www.ncbi.nlm.nih.gov/pubmed/19389130

Gómez-Pinilla, F. "Brain Foods: The Effects of Nutrients on Brain Function." *Nature Reviews* 9, no. 7 (July 1, 2008): 568-78.

Grohol, John M. Book Review. "Key to Greatness Is Working Memory, Not Practice." *Psych Central* (October 6, 2011). http://psychcentral.com/news/2011/10/06/key-to-greatness-is-working-memory-not-practice/30110.html

Halber, Deborah. "Sleep Helps Build Long-Term Memories." *MIT News*. June 24, 2009. http://web.mit.edu/newsoffice/2009/memories-0624.html

Kiewra, K.A. "Note Taking and Review: The Research and Its Implications." *Journal of Instructional Science*. 16 (1987): 233-249.

Locke, Edwin A. and Gary P. Latham. "Building a Practically Useful Theory of Goal Setting and Task Motivation: A 35-Year Odyssey." *American Psychologist*. 57 (2002): 705-717. http://faculty.washington.edu/janegf/goalsetting.html.

Ordonez, Lisa D., Maurice E. Schweitzer, Adam D. Galinsky, and Max H. Bazerman. "Goals Gone Wild: The Systematic Side Effects of Over-Prescribing Goal Setting." *Harvard Business School NOM Unit Working Paper* No. 09-083. 3 (January 23, 2009). http://www.hbs.edu/research/pdf/09-083.pdf

Roediger, Henry L. III, Kathleen B. McDermott, and Mark A. McDaniel. "Using Testing to Improve Learning and Memory." Washington University in St. Louis. In press (2007). http://psych.wustl.edu/memory/Roddy%20article%20PDF's/Roediger_McDermott_McDaniel_inpress.pdf

Seijts, G. H., and G. P. Latham. "The Effect of Distal Learning, Outcome, and Proximal Goals on a Moderately Complex Task." *Journal of Organizational Behavior*. 22 (2001): 291-302.

"Setting Objectives." *Focus on Effectiveness: Research-Based Strategies. Northwest Educational Technology Consortium*. Dec. 3, 2011. http://www.netc.org/focus/strategies/sett.php

Siemens, George. "Learning and Knowing in Networks: Changing Roles for Educators and Designers." Presentation at the ITForum, January 27, 2008. http://it.coe.uga.edu/itforum/Paper105/Siemens.pdf

Suzuki, Shunryu. *Zen Mind, Beginner's Mind: Informal Talks on Zen Meditation and Practice.* New York: Weatherhill, 1994.

Yates, Diana. "Physical Fitness Improves Spatial Memory, Increases Size of Brain Structure." *News Bureau Illinois.* February 25, 2009. http://news.illinois.edu/news/09/0225memory.html

10 Ways to Be a Better Learner is a great resource to offer to attendees at seminars, educational meetings, and conferences. If you are interested in receiving a discount on a purchase of 15 or more copies, send an e-mail to books@missiontolearn.com indicating the number of copies desired.

About the Author

J eff Cobb is an avid lifelong learner and, through his firm Tagoras (www.tagoras.com), a highly sought after adviser to organizations in the business of continuing education and professional development. He is the co-author of *Shift Ed: A Call to Action for Transforming K-12 Education* (Corwin, 2011) and author or co-author of numerous books and reports on trends in the field of continuing education and professional development. He blogs regularly at www.missiontolearn.com as well as at www.tagoras.com/blog/.

Jeff speaks frequently on how businesses, trade and professional associations, and other organizations are being impacted by the shift towards a "learning economy." If you are interested in having Jeff speak at an event, contact him directly at jtc@jeffthomascobb.com.

Shift Ed: A Call to Action for Transforming K-12 Education

In *Shift Ed: A Call to Action for Transforming K-12 Education* (Corwin, 2011), Jeff Cobb collaborates with futurist David Houle to issue a "call to action" to all of us who are concerned about education in America.

Starting from a brief overview of the history of education in the United States, the authors paint a compelling picture of the forces that are driving us towards an inevitable – and transformational – shift in how we approach educating our children. Core to the authors' argument is a belief that we already know what we need to know to transform education – we simply have not chosen to act as we need to.

Shift Ed is not just a book for educators. Its message is directed at anyone who cares about the future of the United States, including parents and grandparents, policy makers, and business executives. It is a resource for sparking debate, encouraging all of us to ask the right questions, and ultimately, spurring us to action.

Find out more today at www.shiftedtransformation.com.

Made in the USA
Charleston, SC
20 July 2012